# BALL PYTHONS AS PETS

## Your Complete Owners Guide

*Ball Python Breeding, Caring, Where To Buy,
Types, Temperament, Cost, Health, Handling,
Husbandry, Diet, And Much More!*

### By Jacqueline Silverdale

D1675106

# Table of Contents

# Introduction

Thank you for purchasing this book! Whether you are someone who has recently made the decision to buy a snake and who wants some more detailed information about your new pet or someone who is simply interested in ball pythons, you will find a lot of interesting and useful information about them within these pages.

Most likely, if you are reading this book, you are considering the pros and cons of getting a ball python as a pet, and you want to find out as much about them as possible. If that's the case, you've come to the right place! There is a lot of information about reptiles in other books and, of course, online, but most of these sources will fall into one of two categories: unreliable or difficult to understand. You need a source of information that is neither of these things, that is both reliable and easy to understand. This book is written for the non-expert, as a simple and direct guide to understanding ball pythons.

After reading this book, you will be in a very clear position to decide if this particular snake is the one for you. It will most probably catch your favor, since it is a docile snake with an easy temperament fine with human handling. It is naturally passive, and will, by nature, hide rather than fight. This character trait makes the ball python a perfect choice for a pet. It is also a robust snake, one that is generally easy to keep healthy. However, this book will also present you with the downsides of ball python ownership so that you will be making a truly informed decision about whether you should get a ball python.

If you do decide to purchase one of these fascinating creatures, this book will help you identify the type to buy, as well as how to feed, house, and keep it healthy. It will also offer tips on breeding, if you are interested. By the last page, you will really be informed about the animal, and any questions you might have had about entering the world of reptile ownership will be answered.

So, go ahead! Get reading and decide if you are ready to become one of the special group of people who own ball pythons!

# Chapter One: About Ball Pythons

If you are planning on getting a reptilian pet, you're going to want the best, right? Ball pythons are the blue bloods of the reptile world. Indeed, they are otherwise known as royal pythons.

The species comes from sub Saharan Africa. Usually, it can be found in countries such as Guinea, Sierra Leone, Liberia, and Ghana, as well as the Ivory Coast. It is not venomous, but rather captures it prey and prepares them for dinner by constriction—that is, it crushes them to death with is powerful, muscled body. Along with other pythons, therefore, the ball python is a constrictor.

# How The Ball Python Got Its Name

You may be curious about how the ball python got its name, especially since we mentioned earlier that it is also known as the royal python.

The scientific name for the ball/royal python is *python regius*, which is where the term royal python comes from. Scientists called this particular python *python regius* because many statues and paintings of Cleopatra depict this species being worn around the royal's wrists. There are also numerous stories of African rulers wearing live royal pythons as jewelry.

So, why are these snakes more commonly known as ball pythons? Well, the common name comes from one the snake's (often considered endearing by owners) habits. When frightened, nervous, or even just sleeping, the python tends to curl itself into a ball. Basically, "ball python" is a more descriptive name in regard to the snake's behavior.

## Appearance

The ball python's build is stocky and it has a relatively small head in comparison to its body. The snake is usually dark brown or black on top, with a pattern that looks like blotches. The scales become light brown or golden as they blend with the underside of the snake, which is typically white or cream, with randomly dispersed black markings.

However, with the growing market for pet ball pythons, many people have used selective breeding to create a number of different varieties, also called morphs, that have significantly different coloring or patterns. The basic description given above simply describes the most common appearance. The next chapter will give a run-down of a number of varieties. As you will see, there are a range of colorings and markings you can select, if you are willing to pay the price.

# Determining the Sex

Knowing whether you have a male of female isn't really all that important unless you plan to breed your snake. But who knows? If little Hannibal turns out to be a female snake, she might not like being called by a decidedly male name.

Determining the sex of a ball python can be a bit tricky, but here are a few tips: Firstly, the male of the species tends to be a little smaller than his female counterpart. The largest females grow to about six feet in length, while males typically grow to no more than four feet in length. Although this might seem pretty long, it is not overly impressive for a python, which is good news, since it means that it won't feel up to tackling a human even if it is extremely hungry. This is actually extremely unlikely in any case; in fact, a dog is more likely to inflict harm than the gentle ball python, but we'll discuss that more later.

Another difference between the male and female are the anal spurs. These are hook-like protuberances toward the tail of the snake. They are, in fact, what is left over from a time when the animal had legs. This time was many, many years ago—millions, in fact—but pythons have still been legless for a far shorter time than most other snakes.

When looking for the anal spurs, be cautious. Right next to them are the anal vents, which, as the name implies, vent the contents of the anus from time to time. You most likely will not have any problems, as snakes poop infrequently, somewhere in the neighborhood of once a week and once a month. Just be aware.

The anal spurs of a male snake are larger and more pointed than those of a female. This is because they play an important part in breeding, but that will be covered in more detail later.

As you may have noticed, the ways to determine your snake's sex are relative comparisons, and as such, may not be very helpful, so if you really need to know (because you plan to breed the python, for example), then it is best to get an expert to carry out a definitive check. This involves looking inside the snake and examining its reproductive organs. Your snake may not particularly enjoy the procedure, but it is the best way to ensure that you know whether your snake is a Phillip or a Phyllis.

## Chapter Summary

In this chapter, we have:

- Discussed how the ball python got its name.
- Learned its most common physical characteristics.
- Discovered how to tell the difference between the male and the female.

In the next chapter, we will cover the many different varieties of ball pythons that you can choose from so that you can decide which one is right for you.

# Chapter Two: Ball Python Varieties

There are many varieties of ball python. Some estimates suggest that there could be over a thousand different ones. In this chapter, we will look at some of the options, both common and rare. We will cover the physical features of each variety, as well as point out any distinctive pros or cons.

Although you would be hard-pressed to find someone familiar with ball pythons who doesn't have a favorite type, they are all wonderful options and have their own merits. To avoid showing any bias, they are presented in alphabetical order:

*Albino Ball Python* – As the name suggests, this is a pale snake, typically bright white with yellow markings, although it can be completely yellow. It tends to have pink or red eyes. As with all albino animals, the albino ball python can be prone to illnesses and skin problems, but it is a stunningly beautiful variety, not to mention extremely popular.

*Axanthic Ball Python* – Like an albino ball python, an axanthic lacks melanin. However, it lacks only red, yellow, or both, resulting in a stunning silver grey and black snake. In case you choose this variety specifically for its coloring, it is important to note that some axanthics' coloring will shift as they get older, becoming browner.

*Blue-Eyed Leucistic Ball Python* – This is a very rare snake indeed (although not as rare as the related black-eyed leucistic ball python), and as such will set you back a hefty amount, depending on how "pure" you want your snake's features to be. The "pure" blue-eyed leucistic ball python is a beautiful snake of complete white color with startling blue eyes. Depending on the genes the snake is bred from, it may end up with slightly different coloring or a few markings. This snake may also be referred to as a "Blue-Eyed Lucy."

*Bumblebee Ball Python* – The bumblebee ball python is the result of a "designer mutation," meaning that it does not exist in the wild. Although there are several different varieties of bumblebee ball

9

python, they all are characterized by yellow and black markings.

*Candino Ball Python* – The candino is similar in appearance to the albino, with stunning gold and white markings, but it is genetically different. While albino ball pythons are made with all albino genes, candino ball pythons are made with other genes in addition to albino.

*Champagne Ball Python* – The champagne ball python is a tan and/or orange snake with irregular stripes and circles along its spine. It also has an all-white belly, which makes it decidedly different from many of the other varieties listed. If you are particularly interested in this kind of ball python, it would be worth taking a look at the pumpkin champagne, a champagne ball python with vivid orange and purple coloring.

*Cinnamon Ball Python* – This brown and cinnamon-colored snake is hardy and inexpensive, making it a great starter snake for someone as of yet unfamiliar with caring for ball pythons.

*Coral Glow Ball Python* – Coral glow ball pythons are remarkably colored, with purple bodies, orange markings, and often, black speckles. However, if you plan to breed your snake, you must be aware that many coral glows have been found to produce only male offspring.

*Fire Ball Python* – Compared to normal ball pythons, the fire ball python is much lighter in color, a brighter pale yellow than brown. When two fire ball pythons are bred, they produce what is basically the Holy Grail of ball pythons: the black-eyed leucistic, a white snake with black eyes and red pupils.

*Ghost Ball Python* – A ghost ball python is created using a recessive mutation that reduces black pigmentation, which gives this snake a hazy, almost spectral, coloring. Hence, its designation as the ghost ball python.

*GHI Ball Python* – Expect to pay a hefty sum for this new kid on the block. A recent discovery genetically, breeders are only just scratching the surface of the different colorings and markings that can be achieved with this snake. The GHI is black and golden brown, with a particularly silky look. This snake has reptile enthusiasts going nuts, which is why some people say GHI stands for "Gotta Have It."

*Ivory Ball Python* – A beautiful white or yellowish white snake, the ivory ball python is produced by breeding together two yellow belly ball pythons, discussed later. They have the same distinctive coloring as the blue-eyed (or black-eyed) leucistic, but with "normal" eyes. They are not as rare, and therefore, not as expensive.

*Lesser Ball Python* – Don't let its name fool you! There's nothing inferior about the lesser ball python. This is another great starter snake, pale to mid-brown and gold, with impressive markings. It is also relatively inexpensive.

*Mojave Ball Python* – Another good-looking snake, the Mojave is brown with striking yellow markings and a contrasting white belly. This is an excellent starter animal, available at a reasonable price.

*Mystic Ball Python* – The mystic ball python is similar in appearance to the Mojave, but with darker coloring. It is a popular snake for breeding, and when mated to the correct partner, can produce a mystic potion ball python, a snake with stunning purple, gray, and pink markings.

*Pastel Ball Python* – This is an extremely popular variety with much more yellow coloring than others. They are beautiful and useful for breeding, as their genes enhance yellow pigmentation in offspring.

*Phantom Ball Python* – The phantom ball python is a lovely black and brown snake with gold markings. It is mainly prized, however, for breeding purposes. Phantoms can be used to produce Blue-Eyed Lucys and purple passion ball pythons, distinctive purple snakes.

*Piebald Ball Python* – The piebald ball python is a remarkable looking snake with areas of pure white. These areas can be few and little more than splotches or many and wide bands. The rest of the snake varies in coloring and pattern. It is highly desirable because of its unique appearance, so expect a hefty price tag if you choose to purchase a piebald.

*Pinstripe Ball Python* – This is a lovely caramel brown snake with stripes along its spine. It is a relatively inexpensive choice, so it makes a good starter snake.

*Spider Ball Python* – The spider ball python is brown and black with a speckled white belly. Its name comes from the spider-like pattern on its back. Because of this unique pattern, it is used in many breeding projects, but it is quite inexpensive, so it would make a great choice for a beginner who still wants something unique.

*Spotnose Ball Python* – This snake has a rather cutely spotted nose, to which it owes its name. It also has a faded pattern on its head and an area several shades lighter than the rest of it along its spine.

*Super Blast Ball Python* – Also known as a killer blast ball python, the super blast is a bright yellow snake with hazy black markings and a lavender head.

*Yellow Belly Ball Python* –The yellow belly is a pretty snake that is most notable for having, as the name states, a yellow belly.


In the next chapter, you will learn about where to buy your ball python, and how much it is likely to cost.

# Chapter Three: Buying Your Ball Python

As with most types of pets, there are many different ways to acquire your ball python. Some of those sources are highly reputable and completely reliable. Some, sadly, are much less so.

A good rule of thumb is to make sure that you can see and handle the snake you intend to buy. You can then check out the conditions in which the supplier keeps their animals. Any reluctance on the part of your pet supplier to do this should raise suspicions in your mind.

Remember, as well, that unscrupulous agents do not usually dress or speak in a suspicious way. They don't wear dark glasses and dirty trench coats. They are often very normal people. You won't always be able to tell a shady supplier from their appearance.

That is why the evidence of your own senses is best. A good supplier will be knowledgeable about their stock. They will keep the animals in clean, appropriate conditions. They will be happy for potential customers to see their stock and handle it.

Another point to bear in mind is that cheapest does not always equate to best value for the money. After all, if your inexpensive snake then has all kinds of health issues, vet bills will soon pile up and you'll end up paying more than you would have for a healthy snake. Plus, if your cheap snake does have health problems and lives only a short while, you'll probably want to buy a new snake, meaning you have to pay the heftier price anyway.

Once again, the best advice is to go and see. The price might be low because the breeder is not concerned with making a ton of money, but rather with finding their snakes the best homes. The price might be low because the snakes are basically off a production line, similar to a puppy mill, where health and safety are not important to the breeder. The only way to know is to check the conditions out for yourself.

# Cost

A number of factors will determine the price of your python. These include the age of the python, its color and patterns, and the rarity of the variety.

For example, the rare Blue- and Black-Eyed Lucy varieties could set you back several thousand dollars. Similarly, because female coral glow ball pythons are much rarer than males, they will be more expensive.

### General Figures

The price of a normal, mature python from a chain pet store is typically between $45 and $80, while a baby python fetches between $50 and $200. Breeders will usually charge between $50 and $200 for their animals.

## Specific Morphs

There are many different types of ball python, so here are listed the typical prices a buyer might expect to pay for some of the varieties. Any figures outside of this range ought to at least raise an eyebrow and prompt a question as to why the cost is as it is.

| | |
|---|---|
| Albino Ball Python | $140 to $450 |
| Axanthic Ball Python | $200 to $850 |
| Ball Python Morphs | $230 to $500 |
| Banana Ball Python | $175 to $650 |
| Bumblebee Ball Python | $100 to $250 |

| | |
|---|---|
| Butter Ball Python | $150 to $375 |
| Candino Ball Python | $320 to $550 |
| Chocolate Ball Python | $125 to $230 |
| Cinnamon Ball Python | $90 to $250 |
| Coral Glow Ball Python | $320 to $570 |
| GHI Ball Python | $2,800 to $4,000 |
| Ghost Ball Python | $75 to $150 |
| Ivory Ball Python | $175 to $375 |
| Killer Clown Ball Python | $1,500 to $2,000 |
| Leopard Ball Python | $85 to $300 |
| Lesser Ball Python | $90 to $160 |
| Leucistic Ball Python | $320 to $450 |
| Mojave Ball Python | $75 to $150 |
| Mystic Ball Python | $170 to $350 |
| Pastel Ball Python | $120 to $250 |
| Pewter Ball Python | $125 to $550 |
| Phantom Ball Python | $120 to $220 |

## Suppliers

Now that you know what you expect to pay for your new pet, we will look at the various places from which you can purchase it.

### Private Breeders

The best place to begin your search is with a private breeder. You will be able to visit (although that might involve a fairly long drive, depending on where your nearest is located). You will also be going to somebody who loves their animals, because they are not breeding commercially, only when the opportunity arises. They are likely to be extremely informed about their animals and much more concerned about the homes their snakes will be going to than the money they will make. Expect to be asked lots of questions. Lots of questions is a good sign.

Even if you don't decide to purchase from a private breeder, visiting one will help you be more informed about purchasing a snake and knowing what conditions they should be living in.

## Commercial Breeders

These people are breeding for business. They are concerned with the money to be made, but this doesn't mean that they do not take good care of their animals. The key is to check reputations, look for reviews, and ask to speak with other customers.

In dealing with commercial breeders, make sure that the snake you see and handle is the one you take away. Most commercial breeders are completely reputable, but take care that you are not caught by one of the few who are not.

## Online Sellers

This is the source that should raise the most questions. If your supplier is online, it is likely to be very difficult to see their animals in person, although many online sellers do provide photos of the snakes they have in stock.

To be cautious, there are a number of questions you can ask regarding the pets:

- *Where are you based, and can a friend or I visit?* Even if a visit doesn't happen, a willingness from the supplier to allow a visit is a good sign. After all, what would they have to lose if they are a reputable supplier?

- *Do you have a list of customers I can contact for a reference?* Expect at least six to be offered. An unscrupulous business owner could have arranged for a friend to be one such reference.

- *How will you transport the snake to me?*

- *Where does your supply of snakes come from?* This is a good question to pair with a request for a visit. If the seller extremely against visits, they may be lying about their methods.

- *Do I have a cooling off period during which you will collect the snake if I am worried about its health?*

- *How long do the eggs incubate?* This is a good question to ask because it is not something everyone will know off the top of their head. An informed, interested supplier should have an immediate answer because they are involved in the breeding process. Someone running a mill will probably need to check before answering. For reference, the answer you receive should be between 50 and 60 days.

Not being able to see and handle the snake you are buying is a drawback to this type of seller. However, good questions and your own instincts can provide you with enough information to decide if a seller is reputable.

You can also check reviews of the supplier, both on their own website and elsewhere on the internet. If you're finding quite a few bad reviews, it's probably not wise to buy from them. Also be on the lookout for false reviews. This is why you should check other places for reviews, in addition to the supplier's site. It is possible for suppliers to stud their own site with fake glowing reviews in the hopes that you will not look any farther into it. If all the reviews on the site are positive, but you find a ton of negative reviews on other sites, the supplier is probably faking their reviews and should be avoided.

## Chain Stores

Obviously, at a chain store, you can see and handle the python you want to take home before you make the purchase. When you arrive, check to see if the animals are all generally in defensive, coiled positions. If they are, that is a bad sign, since it indicates that the snakes are stressed. Now, some may be coiled into a ball to sleep, which is perfectly normal, but at least one or two snakes should be uncoiled and relaxed.

The advantages of a chain store are that it is easy to find lots of online reviews of their services and they will need to be meeting at least minimum standards of care. But, of course, it is a chain store, not a specialist pet supplier, so the knowledge of the staff is likely to be general at best.

**Local Independent Pet Stores**

As long as it is a well-respected place, then an independent store is a good bet. It is still worth asking about the supply chain, and you should definitely ask to handle the snake before you buy it. Being able to visit means that you will get a good idea about the way the animals—and not just your potential purchase—are kept.

You might have to pay a little more than from an online or chain store source, but this should be mitigated by knowing that a local store lives on its reputation. If that gets damaged, then the store is soon likely to be out of business, so it should be doing its best to care for its animals and please its customers.

The only downside of a local independent pet store is that, like a chain store, it is a general outlet, rather than one specializing in snakes.

**Specialty Pet Suppliers**

By this, we mean independent specialty reptile shops. You are likely to pay a premium for buying from a place like this, but the plus is that everything you need, including expert advice and back-up information, is there under one roof.

As with all types of suppliers, remember the three Rs—references, reviews, and reputation—but a reptile store is a safe place from which to buy your ball python.

**Friends and Neighbours**

Clearly, as they are friends and neighbours, you know and trust them. The downside of getting your python from this source is that you will need to be quite lucky to be buying at a time when they have some for sale.

## Chapter Summary

The key messages from this chapter are:

- It is always best to see and handle your potential new pet.

- Prices will vary based on a few factors. Just remember that cheapest is not always the best, but neither is most expensive.

- Check all suppliers' reputations and reviews—and ask for references.

The next chapter will teach you the basics of caring for your snake.

# Chapter Four: Caring For Your Snake

For those who are unfamiliar with snakes, the idea that having a snake as a pet is easy is common. Nothing could be further from the truth. Although snakes don't need to be walked or taken outside, snake owners are just as busy taking care of their pets as other pet owners, ensuring their snakes have an environment in which to thrive.

## Temperament and Handling

As we have mentioned before, the ball python is an extremely docile pet. It is the perfect introduction for an individual or family looking to branch out into the world of reptiles. It can even help teach children about snakes and keep them from developing unfounded fears.

Ball pythons won't bite (unless severely provoked). They aren't venomous, and even though they are constrictors, they are much too small to do any damage to humans, not that they would even try. They fit none of the stereotypes attributed to snakes, which make them both great pets and great teaching tools.

Ball pythons are not slimy to the touch, so you should not feel uncomfortable handling them. In fact, a pet ball python should be handled so that it gets used to human touch. It will tolerate this happily, although will get bored of the attention quite quickly. Ball pythons are inquisitive, intelligent creatures, so don't be surprised if your new pet wants to ditch the cuddling and explore after a while.

## Feeding

Snakes are carnivores. Their general diet consists, in captivity, of mice or rats appropriate to the size of their mouths. A hatchling will start on baby mice about once every five or six days. As it grows, it will move on to adult mice, which it needs to eat about once every seven to ten days.

If the idea of feeding your snake a wriggling mouse makes you nauseous, there's good news. It's actually better not to feed your snake live mice. A live mouse could fight back and bite your pet. Even more dangerous is to use wild rodents, because these could be covered in ticks, mites, or other parasites.

The best option is to feed your python frozen mice. Don't worry about getting the mice. It might sound like a strange product that will be difficult to find, but they are available in most pet shops and online. You can't feed your python the mice while they are still frozen, though. They should be thawed to room temperature before feeding.

Adult snakes can have a bit more variety in their diet. Day old chicks are a good option, although distinctly not for the squeamish or especially soft of heart. As the snake gets bigger, larger mice and rats can be introduced to its diet.

It is also best to take the snake out of its tank for feeding. If you don't, your pet could ingest something it's not meant to, which could become impacted inside its digestive tract. This could cause severe distress or even death, so be careful to prevent this from happening.

Just as people might like to take a nap or lounge about after having an especially large meal, your snake needs to rest after eating. Snakes digest their food extremely slowly, so it shouldn't be handled for at least forty-eight hours post feed, or it is likely to regurgitate the meal.

Rather like young children, ball pythons are really fussy eaters. There are many reasons why they might refuse to eat. Females might refuse to eat if they are about to begin ovulation. They might also refuse to eat if they are about to shed their skin (more on this in the next section). If they are stressed or are being handled too often or if the conditions of their environment are not right, they may also refuse to eat.

One way to tempt your snake to eat is to "brain" its food. This involves cutting into the skull of the prey to release the scent of the brain, which, to the python, is evidence of a gourmet meal.

If that doesn't work, it's okay. It is not the end of the world if your python misses a meal, but you should try to work out why it is not feeding and resolve the matter in time for its next dinner.

Your snake also needs to drink, so make sure you provide it a good-sized bowl of fresh water. It needs to be a solid bowl, or it will tip over when the snake drinks. As we will see next, the water can also be useful for skin shedding, so don't be surprised to see your pet using it as its own private swimming (coiling might be a better word) pool. Because of this, however, you need to keep an eye on the water. If dirt, feces, or other debris is evident in the water, it needs to be replaced, and the bowl thoroughly cleaned.

## Shedding

Pythons will shed their skin several times a year, with the young doing this more frequently than their older brethren.

There are signs which indicate that your pet is about to do this (the proper name for the process is preecydsis). The first clue is that the snake's skin color will change. It will become duller than usual. The eyes of your pet will turn a blue-grey colour, and it will become lethargic. This stage is referred to as being "in blue," and is one of the few times when care needs to be taken in handling the snake.

It is vulnerable at this time, as its vision becomes impaired, so it might become defensive. It is best not to handle the animal as it goes through the shedding process. At this time, most pythons won't eat, but that is not always the case. It depends on how the snake reacts to preecydis.

Some snakes shed easily and without any help, but most can do with a bit of human assistance. Raising the humidity in your pet's tank is one of the most useful ways of doing this. Providing your snake with a larger bowl of water will both increase the humidity and allow the snake to soak if it wants to. Misting the tank also helps to raise humidity.

You can also give your snake a homemade humidity box. This can be something like an ice cream container filled with damp moss. A hole is cut in the top of the box, smaller than the snake, to allow the humidity to escape into the vivarium.

When the preecdysis is complete, the snake enters the ecdysis, or shedding, stage. It will usually start by rubbing its head on a stone, rock, or whatever décor you have inside the tank, to start loosening the skin around its head.

Once its head gets out of the old skin, it will crawl out of the rest of the shedded material, rolling it inside out in the process. A branch or sturdy plant can help it with this. When the snake is completely out of its skin, the old covering should be removed from its habitat.

At that point, it is worth giving your pet the once over, checking particularly that skin over the eye caps and tail has not been retained. Bathing the snake and removing any bits of old skin left will help to avoid infection. This also removes the risk of healthy skin dying under its old coat.

## Written Records

At this point, it is worth pointing out the value of keeping a written and pictorial record of your snake. Diagnosing illnesses can be tricky, since the ball python is a notoriously poor eater, and that is the usual clue to any animal being unwell. A record, in writing and photos, can help to determine changes to behaviour and appearance. In particular, records should be kept of eating habits, shedding habits, and, for females, ovulation trends. It is also worth checking and recording weight and length periodically.

## The Best Kind of Home

Although they can grow to be quite large, the ball python is toward the end marked "lazy" on the spectrum of snake activity. This means that it does not need a large home. A medium-sized vivarium, or even a large fish tank with a tightly fitted top, will suffice. In fact, a smaller home helps it feel more secure. An average-sized adult ball python, perhaps four feet in length, will prefer a home three to four feet long, two to three feet wide, and a couple of feet high.

Note that the comment about the tightly fitted top is especially important. The snakes are very strong, and will push off tops that are not clamped down if the mood takes them.

Inside the tank or vivarium is firstly the substrate. This can be one of the following:

- *Beech chippings* – These look smart in the tank and can be purchased in different sizes, so you can choose the best for your snake. It is great for cleaning, but if your python proves to be a burrower, then it isn't the best option.

- *Aspen bedding* – This is great for most pythons, but it does come with some problems. The animal cannot be fed in that environment, as it may consume the shavings along with its prey. Also, unlike beech chippings, it cannot be cleaned. Urine and feces can quickly coat the bedding and may pose health risks to your snake. When this is the case, the aspen affected needs to be replaced. There should be a full change every month or so in any case.

- *Coco or orchid bark* – Sometimes, shops will recommend this for your snake, although it is more appropriate for snakes that require the highest of humidity levels. It poses no threat to the python, though, so it will work.

- *Artificial grass, or AstroTurf* – This is perfect, as it is easily cleaned and there is no need to look beyond the cheapest version available. Note that you will be able to buy it more cheaply online or at a garden centre than in a specialty reptile shop.

- *Paper towels* – These work, and are great if the animal is in quarantine or healing injuries.

- *Newspaper* – This is often used, although the ink can be harmful to some animals. It is a cheap option, and can be used for very short periods, but it is not an ideal solution.

A little warning: sometimes redwood or cedar chippings are recommended. These are toxic, and for predatory animals, such as snakes, present a significant risk. Avoid these at all costs.

In order to avoid your pet becoming stressed (or in case it does get stressed), a couple of hiding places are recommended. Specially built reptile hides can be purchased, and these are cleanable. However, your pet doesn't care what the decorations look like, so if you aren't overly concerned with appearances and want to take the less expensive route, a couple of cardboard boxes work just as well. Don't pick something that is too large. The animal will feel far more secure in a space just large enough for it to curl up in.

Keep one hiding place at the warm end of the tank and one at the cooler end (we'll discuss why the tank needs two different temperatures in a moment) to give your pet python a choice of where to hide. Keeping hides at either end of the temperature range is very important. The instinct for the snake to hide is stronger than its instinct to keep its body temperature correctly regulated. This means that it can lose control of this, leading to digestive problems and even more serious illnesses and complaints. Making sure it has options to hide in whatever space is best for its body temperature regulation is important.

As well as aiding the snake the shed its skin, plastic plants and branches can provide the snake with places to climb and rest. These can be natural, but must be debugged if from the local woods or your garden. To do this, soak the plant or branch in a chlorine and water solution, then dry in the sun. It is best not to use live plants, but if you do, they should be purchased from a specialist, as many can be harmful to the sensitive python.

As we said earlier, the ball python is an intelligent animal. It likes a change of scenery. Therefore, periodically change the inside of its vivarium. It will be interested in exploring its new surroundings.

# Staying Warm

Ball pythons are cold blooded, and get heat from their environment. In the wild, they bask in the sun, moving to a shady spot if they overheat. In the vivarium, the best range of heat is from 26 to 33 degrees Celsius, or 80 to 91 degrees Fahrenheit. You will want to make sure that one side is warmer than the other, to mimic the snake's natural environment. Your snake may feel too warm on one side and need to cool down, or it may get too cool in one area and want to heat up.

The best way to heat your pet's tank is with ceramic heater with a bulb guard. The bulb guard is important, because while you or I would know very quickly if we touched a red-hot bulb, the snake does not, and severe burning can occur. Either an infra-red or normal bulb can be used, as long as it is fitted with a dimming tool. The dimming tool is crucial, because the animal will become stressed if it has too much light, although it needs a constant source of heat. It is best, just as with humans, to run the light on a normal night/day schedule. Keep an eye on the heat inside the vivarium, with a couple of thermometers placed near the two hiding places, as these are where the python will spend the majority of its time.

A hydrometer is also a must. The snake will thrive at a humidity level of 50 to 60%, and the hydrometer will monitor this. Damp moss, such as in a humidity box described in the shedding section, can increase humidity, and extra vents can reduce it as needed.

## Chapter Summary

In this chapter, you have learned about looking after your new pet.

- You now know about the ball python's diet—mice or rats, about once a week—and some reasons why your snake might refuse a meal.

- You are informed about skin shedding. You know several ways to help your snake along in the process.

- You have learned about proper housing for your snake, including the importance of cleanliness, temperature, and humidity.

In the next chapter, we will look at some of the common ailments your snake might face.

# Chapter Five: Common Health Issues

In this chapter, you will learn about the most common ailments from which the ball python suffers. Remember, if you follow the advice on feeding, housing, and keeping stress to a minimum outlined in the previous chapter, the risk of your snake becoming unwell is much reduced. There are, however, three conditions to which they are prone.

## Regurgitation

This refers to the snake throwing up its food before it is properly digested. As we mentioned earlier, two common causes of regurgitation are stress and handling after eating.

A one-off regurgitation is not a major problem. The important thing is try to identify the cause of stress and make sure that it does not happen again, or if handling was the issue, avoid handling the snake after eating again (unless it is to simply place it back in its tank).

However, regurgitation can be a sign of a larger digestive or general illness. Therefore, even if you suspect the reason for this action is stress or handling, you should monitor it carefully for at least a month following its last regurgitation.

It is also a wise move to give it about a week to settle down following regurgitation before attempting to feed again. If you notice excessive weight loss or any other significant change to its normal behaviour, you should seek medical attention for your pet as soon as possible.

## Respiratory Infections

As hardy as your pet may be, respiratory infections are not uncommon.

Symptoms are as follows:

- Production of excessive saliva
- Production of nasal discharge
- Appearance of wheezing while breathing
- Holding the mouth open while breathing
- Lack of appetite
- Lethargy

Note that respiratory infections can be passed from snake to snake, so if you suspect that your ball python is suffering from one of these, make sure that it does not interact with other pet snakes you may own.

The condition is usually caused by poor cage hygiene, which allows bacteria to form and grow. Excessive humidity in the vivarium is another factor. The vivarium is a breeding ground for bacteria, so make sure it is cleaned well and regularly. If excessive humidity is the problem, then an extra vent or two needs to be purchased for the tank in which your snake lives.

A mild respiratory infection will problem go away by itself. Still, you should monitor your snake carefully. A serious infection can be dangerous, and can also lead to mouth rot, which in turn leads to further problems, such as a reluctance to eat and additional infections. If the infection persists, your veterinarian may prescribe an antibiotic for your snake.

## Mites

These are tiny black parasites that live on your ball python and feed off of its blood. They often gather around the mouth and eyes, but may also creep under your pet's scales. The symptoms to look out for are an increased lethargy and a reluctance to eat.

If you discover mites, your snake needs to be bathed in a tub of warm water. Then, the entire cage needs to be cleaned and disinfected, including hides and climbing features. The substrate will need replacing.

Before putting your snake back into its tank, cover the bottom with white kitchen roll and keep furniture to a minimum inside the vivarium. This helps in two ways. Firstly, any mites will be easy to spot against the white background. Secondly, it helps to prevent breeding. Mites need substrate in which to lay their eggs.

It is possible to get treatment for mites from a reptile shop or a veterinarian. However, repeated bathing and changing of the towels will also clear the problem in most cases.

# Chapter Summary

In this chapter on the health of your pet, we have identified the following three most common ailments from which ball pythons suffer, what causes them, and how to handle them.

- Regurgitation
- Respiratory Infections
- Mites

The next chapter will help you understand snake breeding.

# Chapter Six: Breeding

There's no doubt that a ball python makes a great pet, but you may get even more satisfaction out of breeding your snake and selling its offspring.

Seeing your pets producing healthy young is a great experience, not only awe-inspiring, but educational to adults and children alike. Another benefit of breeding is that, when you sell your snakes, you can make yourself a little bit of pocket money.

## Finding Homes

Before embarking on a breeding program, make sure that you have homes to which the snakes can go. As much as you might love your python(s), everyone has a limit to how many of the slithering creatures they want in their home. Sure, one or two is manageable, but a half dozen might be a bit much. Also remember that although reptilian pets are growing in popularity, they are still quite a niche market, and it might mean hanging on to the hatchlings for a while unless you have already lined up homes for them.

## Preparing Yourself for Frustration

To put it nicely, ball pythons are not rabbits. The females are extremely particular about their partners and the males aren't very aggressive in the matter, probably since the females could have them for lunch if they wanted. It can also be attributed to the fact that the very laid-back nature of the ball python (which makes it such a safe pet to own) means that quite often the male would rather just lay in the warmth than get up to any hanky panky.

More seriously, there is also quite a high mortality rate among hatchlings. You should keep this in mind if you are soft-hearted or if you are involving children in the process. You will need to understand and explain to others that it's possible the babies will not make it.

## Identifying Ovulation & The Process Leading up to it

Identifying when female ball pythons are ready to make can be tricky. The snakes originate from the equatorial regions where temperatures are fairly consistent, so it seems as though air pressure might be the trigger for the breeding process to start. Pressures typically being to drop in the fall, October or November, in the northern hemisphere.

A good sign that the females are getting ready to breed is that they start to eat greater quantities of food. They become extremely animated when food is around, and pet owners need to take a little more care when opening their tanks.

It is best to wait until a female is one and a half kilograms or a little over three pounds before breeding. They can breed smaller than this, but when successful, pregnancy and birth take a lot out of the snake, and a lot of weight is lost. If the reptile doesn't have enough body weight to cope with this, then there is a risk that the animal could be lost.

Early in the new year (in the northern hemisphere), is the time to look to pair the snakes ready for breeding. It is important to check that the female is ovulating, or the (often) reluctant males will waste their time. Ultrasound can be used, or visual clues can be employed.

A female that is nearing ovulation will tend to want to head for the coolest end of the tank, and will "bowl wrap," which is the process of wrapping their bodies around their water bowls, probably for the coolness and pressure. They will become brighter in color, glowing in fact, and will show little interest in their food. Finally, when palpitating them, it should be possible to feel follicles, about the size of marbles, under the skin. These follicles are the unfertilized eggs. They will get bigger the closer the female gets to ovulation.

The female needs to be checked regularly, because ovulation occurs only for about twenty-four hours. Signs are clear, with the female developing a hard midsection and the tail scrunching up.

## The Mating Process

You will actually want to begin pairing your male and female before ovulation so that they can get used to one another. The best bet is to introduce them in the fall and allow them to mate once a month, every month leading up to the female's ovulation.

At the point that the female appears to be ovulating, introduce the male once again. It is best to do this at night, since the snakes are more active at this time.

It is at this point that the male's spurs come into play, gripping and stimulating the female. Look for a lock, when the two animals join together, wrapping themselves around each other. Mating is not a quick job, so this may not happen immediately. Give it three days before declaring the event a romantic failure. Also, when mating occurs, it usually takes several hours, even as long as a day.

When it is over, take the male away for some food and relaxation.

And that is that, at least as far as the male is concerned, and he can go back to a life of lying serenely in the heat of his tank, job done for another year. For the female, though, there remains a lot to do. It will be about fifty days before she lays her eggs, and she will undergo a skin shed in this time. A clue that she is successfully pregnant, or "gravid," will be seeing her lying at the warm end of her tank, seeking out heat and humidity.

## Preparing The Egg Box

Prior to your python producing, an egg box should be placed in the tank. This needs to be a good-sized container with any handles removed, so the snake doesn't get stuck in it. In the wild, the snake would find somewhere warm, dark, and damp, so these are the conditions you need to replicate. For a python, something like a child's toy crate is the ideal size. It should be filled with peat or compost, and some vermiculite from the pet store or garden centre (which will be cheaper!).

## Laying Eggs

There will be lots of clues that she is ready to lay. Firstly, she will change her body shape, becoming triangular. In the day or so before laying she will be restless (wouldn't you, if you were full of large eggs?) and will frequently lie twisted. This is normal, and helps to get the eggs aligned for delivery.

When her tail appears in the centre of her coil, she is probably about to lay. A female ball python typically lays a clutch of six to eight eggs, sometimes as many as ten. She will coil around them once laying is complete, and if any have been laid unfertilized, she will roll them away from the group.

However, it is worth checking these, because she doesn't always get it right. Checking is done by turning down the lights and shining a light on the egg. A series of red veins will be visible if the egg is fertilized. Put it back among the group if this is the case.

You will want to be careful when getting near the female and her eggs at this time, as she will be protective of them and can get pretty nasty.

# Removing the Eggs

Your friendly python might not be too keen on having her eggs removed, even for their own good. She could hiss and strike to protect them, so movement from your side has to be quick, keeping stress for the snake to a minimum. Carefully, grasp her behind the neck and at the base of the tail, uncoil her, remove the eggs, and then place in her a warm bath.

This will help her forget the eggs, as their smell will be removed. She will get back to feeding—which is important because a lot of weight will have been lost—more quickly that way. While she is bathing, clean out the tank, replacing the substrate. This too will take away the smell of the eggs and get her feeding more quickly.

Your snake may still go back to the egg box to be with her eggs. If she has laid in the box with the eggs for a few days, then check that she hasn't buried the eggs (they need some air) and that the mixture hasn't dried out. Also, when moving the eggs, make sure that they are laid in the same position in the box, as they do not like to be rotated. Sometimes, they will be laid as a clump. That is fine, they will separate of their own accord when the time is right. It is also a good idea to place pegs or straws around the eggs to stop them from rolling, because if they do, the yolk and embryo may separate, killing the unborn python.

# Hatching

The eggs—which are not, by the way, completely smooth like birds' eggs, more like white potatoes—will take about 50-60 days to incubate, usually around 55. After that, with a little luck and lot of care regarding temperature, darkness, and moisture, you should find a lot of little wrigglers have been born.

In terms of eating, the new babies will have a similar diet to their parents, just smaller versions. Baby mice are a common option.

## Chapter Summary

In this chapter, we have covered the breeding process, including

- How identify ovulation
- How to introduce the male
- How to prepare an egg box

- How to remove the eggs from the female

- How to keep the eggs safe during incubation

The last chapter will help you form a step-by-step plan for purchasing and enjoying your new pet ball python.

# Chapter Seven: Action Steps

In this chapter, we will look at the process a prospective ball python owner should go through in order to become a fully-fledged snake person.

We have saved this chapter for last because you are now informed enough about the ins and outs of ball python ownership that you can make the proper decisions.

## Planning

This is the first thing you need to consider. You have already made a start on this, by reading this book, but do your research about snakes in general, and reptile ownership, as well. Find out about clubs you could join, and where other local owners are situated.

Sharing of information is always good, and having an independent source of discussion, where your expert is not also looking to sell you something, is a very good idea.

Reptile owners are proud of their pets, and happy to talk about them. They will often be found at fayres, craft shows, and animal shows, keen to chat about husbandry and health for their animals. Don't be afraid to seek members of this community out. You can even start small by posting in an online reptile forum.

## Questions

The next step, once you have decided that you are really keen on owning a snake, is to ask yourself a series of questions. The idea of bringing a snake into your home can seem like a good idea, but for some, the potential problems might dilute that appeal quickly. If you can honestly answer the following questions and still have no issues, then you are ready for passage to the next stage of the process:

*Where will I keep my snake? Will this present any problems?* – Remember, a ball python vivarium does not have to be large, but it does need to be secure.

*Do I have young children or other animals who might stress the snake because they do not understand it?* – A "yes" here is not the end of the story, provided you can find a way to protect your youngster from provoking your pet and provide a secure home for the snake where it will not be bothered.

*Do I have somebody to look after it when I am away?* – A python is not like a dog, it does not need a constant companion. But it will need feeding, watering (daily), and tank cleaning. Do you have a friend comfortable with snakes and happy to carry out those tasks?

*Can I cope with dead mice in the freezer?* – It may seem like a silly question, but it is an important one. Some people find such a thought disgusting. You may be okay with it, buy how will the rest of the family feel? This leads to the next question.

*Will my family and friends cope with a snake in the house?* – We could find no examples at all of a ball python seriously injuring or even killing a human. The same cannot be said for certain breeds of canine companion. However, snakes seem to be a part of our collective consciousness, and many people are (wrongly) scared of them. You would not want a situation where a family member is constantly stressed or spends their week worrying about the snake escaping or attacking them when out of its cage when, for example, having its weekly feed. Equally, you would not wish to become socially isolated because your best friends will no longer visit. Almost always, potential problems such as these can easily be solved—for example, by hosting in another room—but the question should be asked.

*Can I make the commitment?* – This is the big one. Your cute little baby python will grow to between four and six feet in length. It could live for thirty years. That is a heavy commitment to take on, and needs consideration. If you have no doubts about answering this question affirmatively, then you are very probably ready to become a reptile owner.

## Equipment and Supplies

If you have decided that you are definitely going ahead, you can choose a spot in your house for your snake to live. And then, it is time to go shopping! We have created a list for you:

- A tank of appropriate size and a SECURE TOP

- Your choice of substrate

- Heating element with dimmer controls and bulb guard

- A hiding place for each end of your tank (can be homemade)

- A humidity box, if necessary (can be homemade)

- A thermometer for each end of your tank

- A climbing feature (can be found in nature and sterilized)

- Artificial vegetation

- A heavy water bowl large enough for the snake to bathe in

You will also need to find a food supplier and make a place for storing the frozen mice or rats in your freezer.

## Buying Your Pet

We have looked at this already in some detail, so will not repeat the options here. We will, however, stress the importance of good research and both seeing and handling the snake you will buy.

## Last Stages

Finally, spend some time finding a network of support, although you may well have already done this. There may be a local club or group that is interested in reptiles. Even if you do not join them, they can be a useful source of information and help.

Find a good vet who knows how to treat reptiles—not all do. There may be periodicals that can be of interest and help, especially until you get more familiar with looking after your snake. Get ahead by identifying friends, neighbours, and family members who are happy to help when you are away from home.

## And Finally

Enjoy your new python pal! We're sure you'll love your new pet!

## Chapter Summary

This chapter has covered the steps you should take once you decide to purchase a ball python. It will help you create a plan of action.

# Final Words

Many thanks again for buying and reading this book! We hope that you are now feeling much more informed about ball pythons, and know whether going out and getting one as a pet is the thing for you. We very much hope it is, because they do make excellent pets!

However, if you have decided that the challenge, commitment, or cost is just too high, you have reached that conclusion based on good, solid evidence, and we congratulate you on that. There are too many animals abused, killed, or abandoned because they were bought on a whim and their owners quickly lost interest. Having taken the trouble to read this book, it is clear that you do not fit into this category.

So, if you do decide to go and buy a ball python, or you have one already, then our final words are simple ones: Have a great time with your new pet!

## Next Steps

Write me an honest review about the book – I truly value your opinion and thoughts and I will incorporate them into my next book, which is already underway.

**Please leave an honest review of my Book !**

If you have any questions at all, please contact me at greenslopesdirect@gmail.com

Thank you!!!

Printed in Poland
by Amazon Fulfillment
Poland Sp. z o.o., Wrocław

32281718R00033